T0413934

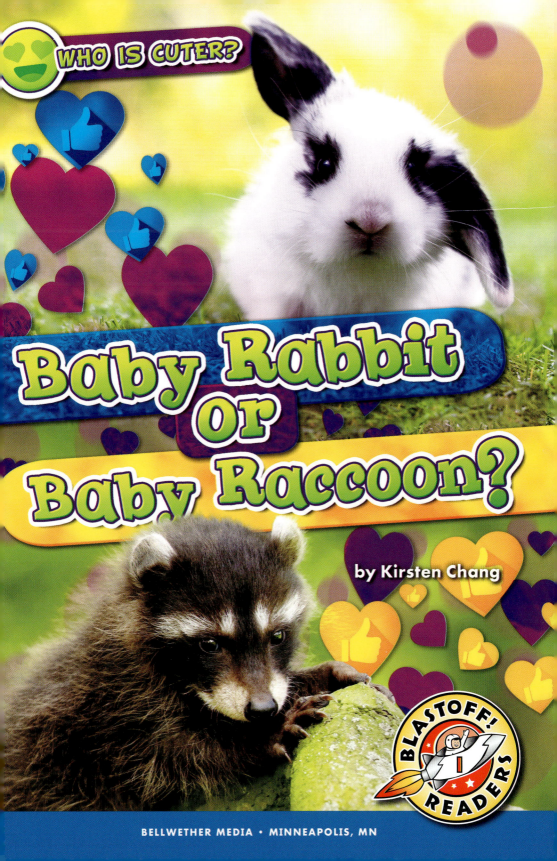

WHO IS CUTER?

Baby Rabbit Or Baby Raccoon?

by Kirsten Chang

BLASTOFF! READERS

BELLWETHER MEDIA • MINNEAPOLIS, MN

Blastoff! Readers are carefully developed by literacy experts to build reading stamina and move students toward fluency by combining standards-based content with developmentally appropriate text.

Level 1 provides the most support through repetition of high-frequency words, light text, predictable sentence patterns, and strong visual support.

Level 2 offers early readers a bit more challenge through varied sentences, increased text load, and text-supportive special features.

Level 3 advances early-fluent readers toward fluency through increased text load, less reliance on photos, advancing concepts, longer sentences, and more complex special features.

★ **Blastoff! Universe**

Reading Level

Grade
K

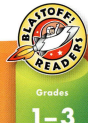

Grades
1–3

Grade
4

This edition first published in 2025 by Bellwether Media, Inc.

No part of this publication may be reproduced in whole or in part without written permission of the publisher. For information regarding permission, write to Bellwether Media, Inc., Attention: Permissions Department, 6012 Blue Circle Drive, Minnetonka, MN 55343.

Library of Congress Cataloging-in-Publication Data

LC record for Baby Rabbit or Baby Raccoon? available at: https://lccn.loc.gov/2024035018

Editor: Rachael Barnes   Designer: Brittany McIntosh

Printed in the United States of America, North Mankato, MN.

Table of Contents

Kits and Cubs!

Baby rabbits are kits. Baby raccoons are cubs. They are cute **mammals**!

kit

cubs

Kits and cubs are born in **litters**. They drink milk from their moms.

litter

mom

7

Fur and Tails

Cubs have mostly gray fur. Some parts are darker. Kits can have many fur colors!

Kits smell with tiny, flat noses. Cubs sniff with pointy, black **snouts**.

snout

Kits have short tails.
Cubs have long,
striped tails.

short
tail ➘

13

Cubs have short ears.
Kits have long ears.
They can point
in many directions!

short ears

Binky and Purr

Kits hop with their strong back legs.
Cubs climb!
They **grip** with their sharp **claws**.

hopping

climbing

17

When kits are happy, they **binky**. When cubs are happy, they purr. Which is cuter?

purr

binky

19

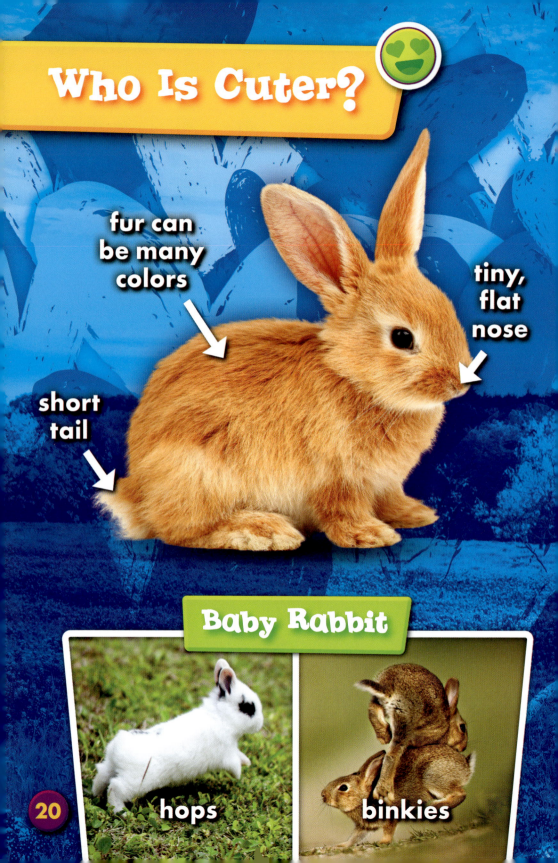

Who Is Cuter?

fur can be many colors

tiny, flat nose

short tail

Baby Rabbit

hops

binkies

purr

Who is your pick?
Vote at
BellwetherMedia.com

pointy,
black
snout

dark
patches
of fur

long,
striped
tail

Baby Raccoon

climbs

purrs

21

Glossary

binky

to jump and twist in the air

litters

groups of baby animals that are born at the same time

claws

sharp, curved nails on the fingers and toes of an animal

mammals

warm-blooded animals that have hair and feed their young milk

grip

to hold tightly

snouts

the noses and mouths of an animal

To Learn More

AT THE LIBRARY

Anderhagen, Anna. *Bunnies: A First Look*. Minneapolis, Minn.: Lerner Publications, 2025.

Chanez, Katie. *Rabbit Kits in the Wild*. Minneapolis, Minn.: Jump!, 2024.

Chanez, Katie. *Raccoon Cubs in the Wild*. Minneapolis, Minn.: Jump!, 2024.

ON THE WEB

FACTSURFER

Factsurfer.com gives you a safe, fun way to find more information.

1. Go to www.factsurfer.com.

2. Enter "baby rabbit or baby raccoon" into the search box and click 🔍.

3. Select your book cover to see a list of related content.

Index